After "I Do!"
A Marriage Map

P. J. LaRue

Acknowledgements

Certain people have made a difference in my life, and without them, I wouldn't have written this book. It is with a grateful heart, that I thank each of you.

First, I would like to thank my Uncle Mike, who makes being loving, positive and encouraging a way of life. Without you, I wouldn't have known that an education means freedom. You were one of the few people who encouraged me when I was young. You told me I was smart and that I could be anything I wanted to be when I grew up. I held on to that advice because it was my lifeline. Your confidence in me led me to go to college and become a CPA.

I would love to tell my dear mom, in heaven, that I am a published author and that I'm very near the top of the ladder at work. Within a few years and more hard work, perhaps I'll be at the top. I believe you can still see me, and you know how hard it was for me to open myself up to the criticisms that come with being an author. And I didn't know that you would be such a large part of this book. I should have guessed it, because you were such a kind and loving person, and such a strong influence on me.

But most of all, I want to thank my husband, my one and only true love, Terry. He is the one who was able to break through my shy demeanor and teach me to believe in myself as much as others believed in me. He gave me true freedom by teaching me about self-confidence.

Introduction

WHEN I ATTEND weddings, I see happy couples who I believe have found their true love. But, as I watch the ceremony, I tend to wonder whether the couple will end up divorced. With marriages in the United States lasting an average of eight years, it's a sad but valid thought. Everyone has heard that 50% of marriages end in divorce. Statistically, it isn't as easy as that to pinpoint the divorce rate, but for the moment, let's just focus on the fact that most couples start out blissfully happy, and way too many end up divorced. And I have not researched the number of unhappily wed couples staying together for "the children."

Over the years, many of our friends have come to my husband and me for marital advice. They came to us because we have been happily married since 1982. Many wanted to know how we do it, and others wanted specific advice about their marriages.

We are proud to say that we have never had a door-slamming fight. However, we have had our differences. It is how we handled the disagreements that kept our marriage alive.

We have some advice that can be shared, but none of it should come as a surprise. This advice is purely common sense driven and when you get down to it, it is also the Golden Rule: Treat others the way you would like to be treated.

People have told us that they think it takes a lot of work to be married. We disagree. It does take effort to learn how to communicate properly, but if you are working that hard, then you aren't communicating properly.

As a preview to our relationship, if we had conformed to statistics, my husband and I would have been divorced long ago because we started our marriage with three strikes against us: My past as the child of an alcoholic parent; the fact that I was a child of divorce; and last, we were quite young when we married.

So while statistically, the odds were against us, after thirty-one happy years of marriage, as of this writing, let's say we beat those odds!

I hope to help you do the same, so I have written about some of our experiences which might help you have as wonderful of a relationship as Terry and I. So congratulations, if you are recently married. Our wish for you is that you'll be on your way to celebrating your silver and gold anniversaries quicker than you know, because time flies when you are having fun.

White Lace and Promises:
The Beginning of Happily Ever After

My Story

I DIDN'T HAVE a childhood filled with innocence or a doting father whom I could wrap around my little finger. He didn't tell me how beautiful I was, and he didn't shield me from the world; in fact, he was the world from which I needed to be shielded, but wasn't.

My father was an alcoholic who sometimes beat my mother. Anger was the first emotion to surface in our family because we lived in a household founded on fights. I didn't learn to express my emotions with maturity because I didn't grow up in a loving, calm and nurturing environment. And because my parents fought first, and sometimes apologized later, I learned to argue rather than discuss disagreements.

This disturbing family dynamic made me distrust men to the point that I'd planned my escape route long before I had a serious boyfriend or fiancé. I had dreams of happily ever after, but that was all they were: Dreams. I thought they were a fairy tale, not reality.

But when my mom left my dad and married my step-father, I saw a couple where respect, admiration and love were the key ingredients. Through watching their love grow, I learned that relationships *could* be happy, and marriages *could* last. I began to believe "and they lived happily ever after" wasn't just a fairy tale ending after all.

I began to open up to the idea that not all men were bad, but my dad's inappropriate behavior was the yardstick in which I measured the characteristics of the men I dated. I didn't date bad boys. Guys had to kind and respectful before I would date them. If they reminded me of my dad in *any* way, I didn't date them.

Although you, the reader, needed to know this about me, dysfunctional relationships aren't what this book is about. I've written about the keys to communication that will help relationships survive because I would love for you to have a relationship as happy as ours.

Terry's Story

TERRY WAS FORTUNATE to be raised in a loving household. His parents married young and were together fifty-one years before his dad passed away. His father, Bill, was a telephone line installer. He met Terry's mom when he was working in her home town. A few months later, when the lines were finished, and he was set to move to the next location, he asked Terry's mom to come with him, as his wife. He was eighteen and she was sixteen. They had Terry a year later. I know what you are thinking, but you are wrong. It was not a shotgun wedding. They were in love.

Bill continued to install telephone lines, which meant that the family moved every six weeks to six months, so Terry was the perpetual new kid in school. As a result, he learned to read people's personalities and to diffuse situations. His education suffered as he changed schools constantly; therefore, the continuity required for learning math skills was broken. Terry later decided he wanted to be an Architect, which meant he needed those lost math skills. He took every level of math while he was in community college. Twice. Except for Calculus, which he passed with a B the first time around. His drive to succeed was there, but he didn't recognize it at the time.

With Terry's parents being married so young, they didn't have much money. Terry has told me stories of his mom collecting soda bottles alongside the road so she could turn them in to get the nickel deposit refund. She used those nickels to buy baby formula for Terry.

The family finally settled into one location when Bill was promoted to a desk job in my hometown. It was there that Terry became an Eagle Scout when he was seventeen. His dad was the Scout Master. Bill required the Scouts to go to experts for guidance when earning their badges. That meant they were taught by the best in their fields of expertise. But it also meant that the Scouts learned respect for those who had mastered their various skills.

Scouting trips in the Appalachian Mountains built his character, as well. Hiking ten miles per day carrying a backpack full of gear and a sleeping bag taught him to be resilient. Getting his fishing badge taught him that he is not a good fisherman, but it did teach him patience. The fish just didn't bite his hook for some reason. Of all the badges that Terry talks about, that is the one he mentions the most. I think that is because he struggled very hard to earn that badge.

Our Story

WE MET WHEN I was eighteen, and Terry was twenty-one. A mutual friend, Chuck, who was home from college for the summer brought Terry to church one Sunday and introduced Terry and me. But Terry thought I was too young, so he didn't ask me out. Even though I was eighteen, I looked about fifteen.

Terry continued to attend church with Chuck throughout the summer, and then they'd hang out at the beach. At the end of the summer, Chuck finally told Terry that I was eighteen and that Terry could ask me out without getting into trouble. But when Terry did finally ask me out, I turned him down because I was in a long-distance relationship with a guy named Mike.

So Terry moved on and began dating another girl. About a month later, the guy I was dating broke up with me. My step-sister encouraged me to ask

Terry out saying, "No one will know that you aren't dating Mike. And you know Terry is interested in you because he already asked you out."

I was painfully shy back then and asking any guy out was absolutely mortifying, whether he was interested in me or not. But my alternative was to sit at home, so I worked up my courage to talk to Terry. Fortunately, Terry came to church even though Chuck had returned to college. I stood before him, shifting from one foot to the other, my voice shook as I stammered the words to ask him out. Fortunately, the girl he'd started dating had also left for college, so he accepted my poorly executed invitation.

When he picked me up for our first date, I felt chemistry so strong that I wanted to kiss him right there at the front door before the date even started. I was too shy, and knew it certainly wasn't appropriate, so I didn't. But when we did share that first kiss, sparks flew for both of us. It was as though our hearts and our bodies knew we were meant for each other before our minds did. We picked our wedding date after six short weeks of dating. The only person we shared our secret with was Chuck. We knew that with both of us being so young, we would receive a lot of grief about our decision. We finally told our families and friends that we were going to be married once we'd dated for six months.

My mom and step-dad, who had both been divorced and remarried, were concerned about our young age, but supportive. They made me promise to finish college before having children, knowing that children could distract me from my goal of finishing my education.

My mom was quite relieved when I told her I was engaged. I used to tell her I would never be dependent on a man. She thought I meant I'd never marry, but what I truly meant was that I wouldn't be trapped in a bad relationship due to financial constraints. While we were lower middle class, I don't remember ever being hungry when I was growing up. But, I do remember my mom juggling bills and using lay-a-way to buy Christmas presents and school clothing.

Terry's parents surprised us by asking what took us so long to get engaged. Since they were young when they were married, they recognized the true love and also knew that young marriages can be successful.

Strike Three Was a Home Run

IN THE INTRODUCTION, the third strike against us was our age. However, when we look back, we think that may have actually been a home run. We finished growing up together, while building our connection at the same time. We came into our relationship with open hearts. Unguarded. Vulnerable. And we handed our hearts to each other on the proverbial silver platters when we walked down the aisle and said our vows. Handing over one's heart is much harder for people who have been through the dating and divorce scene.

I'll admit my heart was probably a bit guarded in that I still feared an abusive relationship like my mom and dad had. I discussed three simple rules with Terry before I agreed to marry him. I told him that I would divorce him if he ever cheated on me, hit me or became an alcoholic. When I think back now, I realize just how low my self-esteem was because I didn't ask for *more*. I did not require that he adore me, make me his princess and treat me like a precious gift. Fortunately, my in-laws raised a true gentleman and that is how he has always treated me. In return, I promised to adore him, treat him like my handsome prince and forever safely hold his heart. When a person is cherished, and the feelings are returned, then the relationship will grow.

Opposites Attract

NOW, I'D LIKE to share some of the advice that we've learned over the years from our friends or family. Opposites may attract, at first; however, the differences between you will eventually cause arguments which will erode your relationship.

Very few of our friends have been able to overcome these differences. The successful marriages we've seen have been built by people who have common interests. They may still have their own side hobbies, and that's fine. But having common activities encourages conversation about the shared experiences.

If your spouse has a particular interest that you don't necessarily share, indulge him or her and attend events together. Then you can talk about what is so appealing about that sport, hobby, etc. Try new activities if you don't have anything in common yet.

You may find that you like something that you haven't tried in the past. We went hiking for the first time in Hawaii and found that we both have a passion for trekking to waterfalls on vacation. We realized we enjoy museums and viewing the art we studied in school. We discovered we love going to the ballet. We found all of these after we'd been married for several years. So don't be afraid to try new things and discover new hobbies, together.

Speaking of loving the ballet, I have to share how that came about. One day I saw that our local company was going to show Cinderella, but we'd never gone and I wasn't sure if I could talk Terry into going. So when I approached him, I was not my normally direct self. The conversation went something like this, "Terry, you know how you like tall, slender, pretty women?"

"Yes."

"How about tall, slender, pretty women that are dancing while wearing tutus? I'd like to go to the ballet and see Cinderella."

"Hey, you tricked me!" he laughed. "Okay, we'll give it a try."

But, that one event allowed us to find how much we enjoy the combined grace and athleticism of the ballet.

And, through Terry's passion for cars, I have discovered that I love to attend elite car shows called *Concour d'elegance* at Amelia Island and Pebble Beach. I even have a favorite car type, the *Delahaye*, previously made in France. And it makes Terry happy that I'll attend these events with enthusiasm. It gives him the freedom to enjoy them, without worrying that I'm bored.

Likewise, my husband helps me proofread blog posts, my children's book series, and offers suggestions for my illustrator. He read this book and provided ideas for topics, as well. I'm pretty sure I like the car shows more than he likes the proofreading, but he does it to help me. (I'm smiling as I write this part because I appreciate his support, and I know I'm getting the better deal here.)

<u>*What Made Our Marriage Last?*</u>

THE PHRASE "STARTER Marriages" didn't exist when we were married. It doesn't just imply permission to bail out; it states it outright. It says, "When I get tired of this man or woman, I'll get a new one." And it tells your spouse right off that you don't believe you are going to make it. That is no way to begin a relationship. If you believe the following, you probably have a starter marriage in the making:

* People do not have soul mates.
* People aren't meant to be together forever.
* If it gets difficult, I can leave.
* It is okay if my marriage ends in divorce.

As opposed to people with the "Starter Marriage" attitude, Terry and I *meant* our vows when we said them to each other. We both committed to the "in sickness and in health" and the "until death do us part" statements with our whole hearts, and that means we don't give up when it gets tough. White lace and promises don't make a successful marriage, and they won't see you through the hard times.

And we have had some tough times. We have seen the passing of my mother and Terry's father, both from cancer. We have seen long periods of unemployment and Terry's enduring various illnesses. But we never felt alone in the storms, because we clung to each other.

These tough times were not in our control. We didn't choose to have periods of illness, unemployment, or to have my mom and his dad pass in such painful ways. But we could choose how we reacted to the situations we were facing, and we chose to be supportive, rather than destructive to each other. We also learned a few things along the way.

My mom's passing from ovarian cancer was the first truly terrible event in our married lives. If I had to look for a silver lining in it, I would say that having eighteen years to build our relationship prior to her passing was key. We'd already learned to communicate and to rely on each other before that.

I learned that my happiness meant everything to Terry, even more than I'd realized. He would have moved mountains to heal my mom for me, if he could have. He had to learn that all he could do was hold me, hug me and let me cry on his shoulder. He felt utterly helpless going through this period because nothing he did could relieve the pain I felt knowing that my mom might not survive. And when she didn't, he was still there, holding me.

One of the most meaningful moments during Mom's illness occurred after she was admitted to the Hospice House and neared her end with us. The family had gathered and was spending as much time as possible with her. It was Father's Day, and we didn't know how much time my mom had left. But Terry also wanted to see his dad and tell him how much he loved him. Terry didn't always say the words, "I Love You" to his parents, but watching my mom passing made him realize he needed to say the words, especially to his dad on Father's Day. Terry had to drive more than three hours to get to his parents' house to have dinner with his dad. Then he turned around and drove back to the Hospice House to be with me. I had an anxious night awaiting his return, fearing that fatigue would overcome him, and he might also die in a car crash.

My learning moment lasted nearly a year as I worked through the anger stage in the grief cycle. I had to let go of the plans my mom and I had made. Mom was my step-dad's caregiver as he had emphysema. She'd planned to move to my new town once my step-dad passed, and we planned to be best friends now that I was an adult. We planned to do all the girl friend things we'd missed because I got married so young. I had to grow past the anger I felt toward the world that she didn't survive. As I'm writing this, I'm still learning. It doesn't surprise me now that my primary reaction back then was anger since that's how I grew up.

When Terry's dad was diagnosed with colon cancer, we both knew he was not going to have much time left with us as the cancer had metastasized, and was discovered as a growth on his skin. I was then relegated to the role of supporter and learned how helpless one feels when his or her true love is hurting with unbearable grief burning into his or her core, and that the only thing to do is hug tightly.

And this last year, Terry has been dealing with several viruses that strike the immune system and short term memory. He hasn't been able to work due to the side effects of the medication. We are making our way through it, and he started applying for jobs, but the doctor told Terry he wasn't healthy enough to get back to work yet. But we have done our best to joke about his memory lapses and look forward to the future.

Certain Rules Cannot be Broken

NEVER ABUSE your spouse. Whether verbal or physical, there is no excuse, no matter how you were raised. Abuse is unacceptable in any form. If you grew up in a dysfunctional household, get counseling if you need it. But, don't use your past as an excuse to continue bad behavior in your present and future. Abuse _is_ a valid reason for divorce.

NEVER CHEAT. Remember your wedding vows! This is paramount. Do not cheat on your spouse _ever_. Even if he or she never finds out, _you_ will know. Would you want them to cheat on you?

My husband I have always been faithful to each other and to our vows. Of course, I see handsome men, and he sees beautiful women, but we have built a relationship that cannot be replaced by a one night stand, or even a longer term fling. There is nothing another person can offer that would make losing our relationship worthwhile.

More than that, we have witnessed the impacts of infidelity on friends' marriages. None survived, even with counseling. The broken trust couldn't be repaired. That meant the cheating spouse always had to explain every minute of a prolonged absence. And the spouse that was cheated on didn't believe the cheater, even when the cheater *was* telling the truth.

TRUST. Always trust your spouse until they give you a reason not to. If it seems like something is wrong, ask about it. Perhaps it is as innocent as planning a surprise for you. However, some partners are not what they should be, so don't be a doormat, either. Use your common sense and know your spouse's normal response.

BE YOUR PARTNER'S BIGGEST CHEER-LEADER. If you aren't it, then who will be? By supporting your partner, you are giving him or her the freedom to grow, learn new things and evolve. Just make sure you are there by his or her side so you evolve together.

I mentioned before that I was shy when I was young. I also had a terrible self-image that didn't change as I outgrew the awkward pre-teen buckteeth, braces and yes, the geeky headgear. Other kids teased that I was so skinny, I had to jump around in the shower to get wet. And I had the huge glasses that were so popular in the late seventies and early eighties. When I was a young girl and would say anything about looks, my mom or grandmother would respond that beauty is only skin deep. Or that true beauty lies within. I don't know why, but they never told me I would grow out of the ugly duckling years or to look past the buckteeth and glasses because they would be corrected by the braces and the contacts. So I truly believed I was ugly.

Terry had told me I was beautiful ever since we met. I put it off to him being in love, and that was what people in love say. I still saw my oversized glasses, buckteeth and eventual braces. One day, Terry was finally tired of my lack of self-confidence and dragged me into the bathroom in front of the mirror.

He gently said, "I'm going to help you see yourself the way I see you." He proceeded to point out that my soft hair glistened as the light fell on it, that I was so pretty I could have been a model, my skin was clear except for a cute sprinkling of freckles across my tiny cute nose, my green eyes twinkled when I looked at him, my body was well proportioned for my small frame and my smile lit my face.

It was that day, when I was in my thirties, that I shed my ugly duckling persona and began to believe in myself.

And I was Terry's biggest cheerleader, too. Although Terry had earned his AA from the local community college, he didn't think he was smart enough to get his Bachelor's degree. Though he struggled in math, I encouraged him to try and emphasized that with the exception of math, he never studied when he was in school. It was a lack of effort that made him earn C's, not that he wasn't smart enough.

I cheered Terry on when he decided to go back to college at twenty-eight with much trepidation. He completed two degrees, one in Marketing and the other in Management. But his 3.8 GPA brought him the President's Honor Roll and membership in the Honor Society.

Don't Wait Until Retirement to Make Memories

HAVE FUN THROUGHOUT your relationship. Find hobbies you both like to share and do them as often as you can. Take pictures, and talk about your experiences. Don't wait until the children have moved out or you retire from your jobs. You don't know when your lovely wife or handsome husband will be taken from you. Tragedies like car crashes and illnesses can strike at any time. Your precious memories will help get you through the tough times.

We learned this nugget from my mom and step-dad. He lived many years with emphysema. When it got too tough for them to go on vacation and drag along all of his medicine, oxygen and other paraphernalia, they looked at pictures and reminisced about the fun things they'd done when they were first married. The happier times were part of the foundation they'd built to help them deal with his terminal illness.

Some of our favorite memories are from hiking trips. The quiet woods allow our minds to shed the stress of city life. And after we reach our waterfall destination, we sit and watch the water and listen to the roar of the water rushing down the mountain crashing into the pool below. And the toughest trails seem to bring the highest reward. A bit like life. The hard times make us appreciate the good times more.

In Sickness and Health

WHEN WE SAID our vows, we knew that heart health and diabetes were an issue for Terry's side of the family. However, we didn't know that he must have inherited every bad gene possible. Our family doctor even told Terry that "you have the genes of a cesspool." Trust me, that is not a statement you want to hear from your doctor.

Terry's health has put our relationship to the test over the years. During 1996, he had appendicitis which resulted in a blood clot. He continued to have unusually severe abdominal pain. An MRI showed he also had a kidney stone. Due to the blood clot, he could not undergo lithotripsy to break the stone into smaller pieces before expulsion. The next two months were a challenge as the stone traveled its painful path.

There were many nights that Terry slept on the couch, as it was softer than our bed. And since the love seat was too short for me to sleep on, I took its cushions to make a bed on the floor to be near him. It didn't seem like it then, but two months was actually a short time to have to deal with a health issue.

About ten years later, Terry's next major health issues began to manifest themselves as a result of his sleeping habits. He could fall asleep, but regularly woke around 3:00 or 3:30 in the morning. When he was young, the energy of youth kept him going. But as he aged, that wasn't the case anymore. The lack of sleep led to burnout causing him to lose his career ambition.

This was the beginning a difficult period for us that has been going on seven years now. Terry has always been a natural leader, but because of his health issues, I began making the majority of the household decisions without the benefit of my partner to discuss issues and any potential ramifications. I felt like I lost my partner and gained a grown child for a long time.

Then, as we were getting the sleep issues under control, Terry was diagnosed with several viruses known to attack the autoimmune system. When the blood work first came back, we thought it was wrong due to the names of the viruses. We focused on herpes and chlamydia, rather than the *non-sexually* transmitted part of the name:

> * Non-sexually transmitted herpes virus, aka HHV6

* Non-sexually transmitted Chlamydia / pneumonia virus
* Epstein-Barr virus
* Mycoplasma pneumonia

But when Terry began to repeat himself, we knew something was wrong. He'd find two or three tidbits of information that stuck with him and he would then tell me about these items two to three times per day. When his next round of blood work confirmed that it wasn't a mix up at the lab, we learned that the memory loss was in direct correlation with the viruses, and that if they'd been left untreated, he would have developed early onset dementia and/or Alzheimer's disease. He is on a drug regimen that makes him feel like a walking pharmacy. I counted his medications at one point, and he's taking twenty-six prescription drugs and vitamin supplements. The sleep issues lasted about two years and have been resolved. But, the viruses were diagnosed in 2012, and as of this writing are ongoing. This will be a battle we face throughout the rest of Terry's life.

As the antiviral and antibiotics did their trick, Terry has become less dependent and much more the person that I met and married. I was overjoyed to see my loving partner return focused, willing and able to contribute, within the confines of his illness and treatments. We know that he may or may not be able to work in the future due to the side effects of the illness and the medication protocol.

So, when you commit to "in sickness and in health," know that it may not be a short illness, like the flu. Our best advice on this is to be loving and supportive. The communication skills you've practiced, along with your commitment to each other, will help you make it through the bad times. And, make it a point to keep your sense of humor. You will need it.

Communication

THERE ARE MANY facets to communication, and it encompasses most marriages' success secrets, or destructive bombs. As I mentioned before, anger was my first emotion, and I didn't know how to control it. My husband, on the other hand, was calm and rational about events. His attitude helped me learn how to communicate in a healthier manner. It takes two to argue, and he wouldn't argue back. It became embarrassing to try and pick a fight, when he'd say, "Come back when you can talk about it calmly."

Healthy communication involves exchanging information without hurting each other. For example, "Honey, are you wearing _that?_ It makes you look fat," is an incredibly hurtful statement. But, "Honey, could you wear your red pants tonight, they flatter your curves," is much nicer. Find ways to say what you need to say in a way that won't hurt your partner's feelings.

Actually, Terry is my clothing judge. Even if he doesn't go shopping with me, when I come home, I try everything on for him. If he approves, then I know the outfit is flattering. But, this is important. He never says I look bad in an outfit. It is more like "the outfit doesn't do you justice." Even at my age now, I love to model clothes for him. When he sees the right outfit, his eyes light up and his face glows with pride. How can a girl (woman) not love *that?* Yes, I still think of myself as a girl sometimes, usually when he throws an adoring look my way.

Communication Tips

* **Honesty** – If you lie to your soul mate, how will he or she trust you? And how do you expect to keep your soul mate happy?
* **Be Open** – The tiny issues lead to the big blow ups. Tell your husband or wife what you need to say before it becomes a huge sore spot. If your spouse has a habit that drives you crazy, like leaving socks in the living room, then say so. Don't let it fester until you throw all of the socks into the trash.
* **Listen** – When your husband or wife tells you that you are doing something that

bothers them, make an effort to change. The small things like socks in the living room build up until they explode. Pick them up and put them in the hamper. Don't let little things become the seeds of divorce.

* **Never Trash Talk** – Don't tell your secrets to your family or friends. Secrets have a way of spreading and you will hurt your spouse if you talk negatively about him or her to your friends. It is, however, okay to enlist help if you are being abused.

* **Don't Play Games** – Okay ladies, admit it. Women love to play games. Raise your hand if you've ever told your husband something like, "You should know why I'm mad!" while giving him the silent treatment. Guess what. Your husband probably does not know why you are angry, and if you don't tell him, the problem will not be resolved.

* **Whisper Sweet Nothings** – Hearing "I love you. You are beautiful," (or handsome), and other sweet compliments never grow old! I bet Terry and I would be millionaires if we had a put a dollar in a jar for each *I love you* and every kiss we've exchanged. And surprises like love notes, or flowers for no reason result in big brownie points. Don't stop doing these

things when you've been married for a while, because they keep the romance alive.

* **Choose Your Words Carefully** – Words *can* hurt and *cannot* be unsaid or unheard. You can apologize, but those hurtful words will always be in the back of your spouse's mind.

* **Change Requires Self-Awareness** – My husband held a figurative mirror up to show me my behavior. And I didn't like the reflection I saw. With his help, I learned something about myself that needed to change.

* **Change Takes Effort** – I had to learn how to communicate in a healthy way. That required a conscious decision to change my behavior. It wasn't easy, but it can be accomplished with practice.

* **Compromise** – Have you ever noticed that promise is part of the word compromise? As in, "I promise to love you and cherish you forever and ever and even into the eons after that." For your love to survive a human lifetime, you will need to compromise during a fight. There is a phrase, "to win the battle, but lose the war." If it is so important that you win each fight, then you will eventually lose your marriage, not that marriage should be a war.

* **Tone** – Be careful how you say what you need to say. Your voice can sound different than your words. The words, "I'm fine," sound different when you say them with a smile versus shouting, "I'M FINE."

* **Body Language** – Let your body language support the words you are saying. People "hear" non-verbal cues from body language as loudly as the words that are actually spoken. Don't send mixed signals. If you tell your partner everything is okay, but your arms are crossed and you have a frown on your face, then your body language doesn't agree with the message you are saying.

* **Golden Rule** – To paraphrase it, treat your true love the way you want to be treated. As the song says, "R-E-S-P-E-C-T."

Our One Brain

OUR FRIEND CHUCK, who introduced us, became a lifetime Navy officer. We often vacationed wherever he was stationed. One particular time, he was stationed in Japan. During this trip, Chuck paid us the best compliment we'd ever received, although we didn't think so at first. He told us we had one brain between the two of us. We had to ask him to explain that comment, because on the surface, it was insulting. But once he explained his logic, we understood what he meant, and we've cherished that comment for years.

We were all out of our comfort zones since none of us spoke Japanese. Chuck told us that he'd been watching us as we dealt with situations that arose on the trip. When I was stronger at a particular task, I would take the lead and Terry would take a supportive position. When another task came up and

Terry was the stronger one, then he would take the lead and I would revert to a supportive role. Chuck said that we did this routinely without discussing who should lead and who should follow.

I can't think of a better compliment for a couple than to know that they are that familiar with each other's strengths, and comfortable with their partner's judgment that they seem to share one brain.

Food Fights

WE COULD HAVE had two rip roaring fights over dinners very early in our marriage, but the events were funny, even right then. Fortunately, we didn't have to wait until time passed to find the humor. The great deviled egg fiasco happened within a week of us being married. Terry had a co-worker who had advised him, "_Never_ say this doesn't taste like my mom's!"

As a wedding gift, my in-laws stocked our spice cabinet and filled our refrigerator while we were on our honeymoon. But they missed the white vinegar. Now, I knew how to make deviled eggs, but substituted a little pickle juice because I was right in the middle of making dinner when I noticed I didn't have any vinegar and couldn't run to the store.

Of course, my husband tasted the eggs, and said, verbatim, "These deviled eggs don't taste like my mom's." He started laughing so hard tears were streaming down his face. I, however, was busy retorting the exact statement his co-worker warned him about, "I am *not* your momma!" I was quite aggravated at his laughter, and was growing more agitated by the minute until he explained the conversation with his co-worker and that the situation had played out just as predicted.

The second near miss in the kitchen occurred with a nuclear meatloaf. Terry likes spicy foods and had indicated he didn't really like meatloaf because it's bland. Before we were married, I'd made meatloaf many times, but with all of the standard ingredients. Trying to please Terry, I decided to try and spice up a meatloaf. I proceeded to open the cabinet and randomly select spices. The outcome was the rankest smelling meatloaf ever known to mankind. Terry held it down in front of the cat to see how she would react. Completely repulsed, fur standing at attention and back arched, she backed out of the kitchen never taking her eyes from the offending meatloaf. Needless to say, the dinner went into the trash, and we went out that night. We've often joked that the meatloaf was the United States' weapon which caused the Chernobyl nuclear meltdown or the fall of the Berlin wall.

I've never made deviled eggs or meatloaf again in the thirty plus years we've been married. I know I can make them, I just don't feel the need. Why ruin two perfectly humorous stories by telling people I now make the dishes using standard recipes?

Division of Duties

SINCE WE'RE TALKING about chores around the house, let's talk about the division of those tasks. This is an area that has come to the forefront since women joined the workforce. If you are both working outside the home, then you both need to share the responsibilities at home. And ladies, you may have to tell your husbands what you need done. Terry is completely willing to help out, but is absolutely blind to the various tasks unless they are about to bite him.

I had a hard time with that concept. I manage a small, but competent and independent staff at work. They do their jobs without being told what to do, and I thought he should do the same when it came to household chores. I thought, how hard is it when most chores need to be completed weekly, and they don't change from one week to another?

This is an area where I had to compromise.

Remember that word? I had to learn that if I wanted help around the house, I needed to specifically list out the chores to be completed. At this time, we are thinking of hiring a maid to help resolve the issue. Terry helps when he can, but his illness makes it difficult for him to contribute, which leaves most of the work for me.

I have learned not to nag! People learn selective hearing in a flash. And don't ask your men to do something during THE BIG GAME. *That* has the potential to create a huge argument. If you ask ahead of time, when it isn't an emergency, then you will most likely get the assistance you requested, and you won't feel like you have to nag to get tasks accomplished. After he does whatever you've asked, you need to thank him. Unfair, you say? He doesn't thank me for what I do! Think of it this way: Would you rather take a minute to express your appreciation and have continued help around the house, or would you rather spend hours fighting about who handles more chores?

And men, don't ignore your wife. She needs your help. What better way to show your love than to ease her tasks? Think about it. She works all day, cooks dinner, cleans the kitchen, helps the children with their homework, bathes them and puts them to bed. By the time she collapses into bed, she's not going to be in the mood for a little fun before sleep. If you help her with these chores, she will be appreciative, have more time and be more energetic.

The Children

THE FIRST THING you need to decide on is whether to have children and how many. This is an important decision that impacts both of you, possibly your careers and your lifestyle choices. And for the kids' sake, make sure _both_ of you want children if you choose to have children.

I do not feel comfortable talking about the topic of children, as we chose not to have any. Therefore, I'm not going to provide any other advice here. Well, maybe one thing. Your relatives still love getting pictures of your children, even in this digital age. So please share freely.

Family and Friends

I AM FORTUNATE that I have a good relationship with my mother-in-law, and Terry says his dad treated me as though I was the daughter, and Terry was the son-in-law. Actually, I did have Bill wrapped around my little finger when Terry and I were first married. All I had to do was say his name with a long, slow Southern drawl, Beeeel, and he'd come running. I usually needed something repaired, and Bill knew how to fix appliances. Of course, I got bumped from my pedestal when the grandchildren came along.

Likewise, Terry adored my mom. So we were both lucky with the in-law situation. Actually, my mom's last words were to Terry. She asked him, "How did you ever get into my heart?"

But let's face it. Not everyone is so lucky with the in-laws, or even some of your spouse's friends. Now, you may not like your spouse's family or friends, but do not deprive them of seeing each other. You can still have girls' and guys' night out. And you can't avoid your in-laws forever. There will be times that you need to get together, such as holidays. Your spouse will appreciate your efforts if you do your best to keep the peace and have an enjoyable time together.

Money Handling

MONEY IS ONE of the areas that couples fight about most. It would be a good idea to lay the ground rules about your finances before you get married. Some couples like having joint bank accounts and some couples like having separate. I think it depends upon the couple.

Also, large purchases need to be discussed and agreed upon. If you are on a tight budget, an unknown purchase could cause payments to be late. And, not conferring with your partner about large purchases is disrespectful. A solution might be to set a dollar cap that both of you can live within, but do not feel constrained, either.

If only one of you handles the money, make sure your spouse has access to information and doesn't feel like you are hiding financial details. Also, make a list of bills that need to be paid, bank accounts, credit cards, etc. Your spouse will need it if something happens to you, and he or she has to take over handling the money.

Terry and I had a joint savings account before we even got married. I decided he was spending too much money on me. (What a problem for a girl to have.) I was in college, and working part time, which meant we'd need to live primarily on his salary. So I started taking his paycheck to the bank each week. I'd deposit most of it and then give him an allowance. I started a small emergency fund so that we wouldn't live completely on a week-to-week basis after we married. We opened a joint checking account once we were married. I've always taken care of the finances; however, he is good about giving me receipts for purchases, so I'm never surprised at the end of the month. Terry strongly believes that separate bank accounts do not show a commitment to the marriage and that it can help hide infidelity if a spouse is cheating.

Unlike Terry, I would advise new couples to keep separate bank accounts. If you later find that you have married an abusive spouse, you will need money to escape. And likewise, once you know that you are safe, you can always combine the accounts later.

It's Okay to Go to Bed Angry

WHEN THE SUN is setting, go to bed, even if you are angry. Regardless of the expression, we've come to an agreement that it _is okay to go to bed angry._ That doesn't mean that you don't say "I love you" and kiss good night, though. When you can talk out the reason for your anger without throwing barbs, you won't hurt your spouse in ways that cannot be taken back. As I mentioned before, apologies don't erase the sting of angry words.

After being together for a while, you learn what issues push buttons. Be mature; don't push them. You can apologize a thousand times, but the hurt will never go away, so stick to the topic of what made you angry while discussing it. Don't let the situation escalate to insults or explosive behavior.

Always remember that this person, who has made you so angry, is still your one true love. Don't kill your love by the way you respond to situations. Be open to hearing his or her perspective, rather than being set with defending your thoughts.

We have learned it is okay to agree to disagree on certain topics where neither of us will ever change our minds. Individuals make their own decisions regarding politics, religion, etc., and respecting their decisions makes the arguments disappear. Don't try to convert your husband or wife to your way of thinking; it will only cause friction. This goes back to the opposites attract statements. If you choose a partner that has different values than you, then you need to respect their opinion.

Free Sex

OKAY, I LEFT this until the end because I didn't want to lose you right at the start of the book. The emotions related to sex are so much more important than today's society makes them out to be. Young people are having sex way before they are emotionally ready for it, and I believe it impacts their relationships later on.

My best advice on the subject of sex is to wait until you find *THE ONE*. And you *will* know he or she is *THE ONE*. It feels different than any other relationship you've had.

If you can, wait until your wedding night to make love. Doing so will add an unquantifiable level of trust, love and connectivity to your relationship. Not sleeping with countless others *is* special. Don't let peer pressure tell you otherwise.

Sex is a bond between two people in love that

helps to make your relationship strong. Old fashioned? Yes, but that is okay. Now that it is out there, maybe our younger generations can think before they act.

Obviously, these are my personal opinions. However, getting to know a person outside the bedroom first gives a foundation to a relationship. I've heard all the statements about checking for compatibility before choosing marriage. And I've heard of the three date rule. To expect sex on the third date is absolutely ridiculous!

This is one time I say withhold sex, but in this case, you aren't playing games. You are making a lifetime decision. So give yourself time to find out whether this person is worth getting to know better. Once you've had sex, where's the incentive to stay together in the early stages?

Can't wait until your wedding night? Okay, wait at least three to six months. During that time, talk to your boyfriend or girlfriend. Discover his or her likes and dislikes. Find hobbies to do together (no, not sex). During this time of discovery, you will learn whether he or she is your soul mate.

And Speaking of the Bedroom

CONNECTING IN YOUR bedroom leads to connecting in the rest of your home. You will find that life does get in the way of sex. Busy work schedules, hauling the kids around town, helping the kids with homework, etc. all cut into husband and wife time.

Over the years, we found that when we made time for sex, we were also more cuddly, loving and complimentary everywhere else. I don't have any fancy statistics to share, only personal experience. Just try it. Set aside time for each other. But while we are on the subject, I have a few other nuggets to share:

* Don't withhold sex as a punishment.
* Actually, practice making time for sex. The more you have, the more the bond between you will grow.
* Don't stop wearing that little black dress to

dinner. And men, find out if she loves the just shaved look or prefers the rugged appearance of the five o'clock shadow. Just because you are married doesn't mean you can stop grooming. Make an effort to keep the romance growing.

* Lingerie is a great gift for both of you. Take him shopping with you and let him see you try on different outfits. If he likes you in it, you'll both have fun taking it off later.

* Hold hands, hug, kiss and say "I Love You" frequently and sincerely. Expressing your love helps keep it alive!

* If there are problems in the bedroom, be sure that there aren't physical illnesses contributing to the situation. And don't make a big deal about it. That will make your partner feel worse and put unnecessary psychological pressure on him or her.

Last Thoughts for a Happy Marriage

ONE OF OUR proudest times came after we'd been married many years. A couple approached us and asked if we were newlyweds because we still looked happy to be together and we were holding hands. We told them how many years we'd been married, and they were quite surprised. I'm happy for us, but I find the statement a little sad because it means that most married couples don't look happy together.

What did you promise your true love when you recited your wedding vows? Can't remember? Go get them. (I'll wait.)

Now that they are handy, read them. Often. Vows are meant to be kept. That's why they are called "vows." You meant it when you said them. They should mean as much or more to you now as they did on your wedding day.

Think of all the reasons you fell in love with your husband or wife that you didn't include in your wedding vows. Write them down and keep them with your vows so that you'll be reminded of all the reasons you fell in love.

To keep your love alive, remember how to communicate in a mature way, so that you don't slowly kill your relationship with the "death by a thousand cuts" method of destruction. Remember, daggers in the heart are to kill vampires, not your true love, so don't throw the daggers.

Say "I'm sorry" when it is needed. No one is perfect. If you don't admit your mistakes and make amends, then how do you expect the love of your life to continue to love and respect you?

Finally, I hope these thoughts help you find a lifetime of happiness like Terry and I have enjoyed.

A Special Request from P. J.

Hi, thank you for reading *After "I Do!" Marriage Map*. I am an independent author, which means I don't have a publisher or agent to help me tell others about my books. That means I need your help. If you were to tell your friends about *After "I Do!" A Marriage Map*, I'd be very grateful. And, if you have a moment, would you please leave a review to help others decide whether to buy my book? Thank you for helping me.

Amazon.com:
www.smarturl.it/AfterIDo

Goodreads:
www.bit.ly/1mu3bNP

Follow me on Twitter:
https://twitter.com/PJ_LaRue

Follow me on Facebook:
http://on.fb.me/RsZf1K

Subscribe to:
www.pjlarue.com

I also write a children's book series called The Mystic Princesses. To view them, please visit my website www.MysticPrincesses.com.

About the Author

P. J. LaRue is married and has a Russian Blue cat named Sasha. P.J.'s favorite vacations include hiking to water-falls. In addition to writing *After "I Do!" A Marriage Map*, which she hopes will help couples have happy and successful marriages, she also writes a children's book series called The Mystic Princesses. She loves to travel and plans to take The Mystic Princesses to different locales in future books. She wants to pass the love of travel to young girls, along with the knowledge that they can solve their own problems.